A MEXICAN CHRISTMAS

BY MICHAEL ELSOHN ROSS

PHOTOGRAPHS BY FELIX RIGAU

Carolrhoda Books, Inc./Minneapolis

To the children and families of Oaxaca who helped us with
this book—muchas gracias! —M. E. R. and F. R.

Editor's note: Traditions of the Christmas season vary throughout Mexico.
This book describes traditions in and near the city of Oaxaca.

Text copyright © 2002 by Michael Elsohn Ross
Photographs copyright © 2002 by Felix Rigau

Carolrhoda Books, Inc.
A division of Lerner Publishing Group
241 First Avenue North
Minneapolis, MN 55401 U.S.A.

Website address: www.lernerbooks.com

Library of Congress Cataloging-in-Publication Data

Ross, Michael Elsohn, 1952–
    A Mexican Christmas / by Michael Elsohn Ross ; photographs by Felix Rigau.
       p.   cm.
    Includes index.
    Summary: Describes the experiences of children during the festivals and religious
observances of the Christmas season in Oaxaca, Mexico.
    ISBN: 0–87614–601–9 (lib. bdg. : alk. paper)
    1. Christmas—Mexico—Oaxaca—Juvenile literature. 2. Oaxaca (Mexico)—Social life
and customs—Juvenile literature. [1. Christmas—Mexico. 2. Holidays—Mexico.
3. Mexico—Social life and customs.] I. Rigau, Felix, ill. II. Title.
GT4987.16 .R67 2002
394.2663'0972—dc21   2001008370

Manufactured in the United States of America
1 2 3 4 5 6 – JR – 07 06 05 04 03 02

CONTENTS

A sparkling parade float on Christmas Eve, which is called Noche Buena in Mexico

SEASON OF FIESTAS

It's time for the Christmas holidays to begin in the city of Oaxaca. This beautiful city in southern Mexico lies in a valley between high mountains. Oaxaca has no snow or ice, but no one here needs winter weather to enjoy Christmas. People mark the season with weeks of colorful celebrations called *fiestas*.

This is a season of parades, delicious foods, and family gatherings. It's night after night of fireworks. It's quiet moments in church and thrills on carnival rides. It's a month for honoring tradition and remembering the past. For the children of Oaxaca, it's one of the best times of the year.

Olivier and Katia have their picture taken in front of a painting of the Virgin of Guadalupe.

Crowds fill the church and nearby park on December 12.

FIESTA OF THE VIRGIN OF GUADALUPE

Olivier sits proudly with his sister, Katia. Like children all over Mexico, they are having their picture taken tonight. Katia wears a traditional Indian costume. Olivier is dressed as Juan Diego, an Aztec Indian who lived during the 1500s.

Juan Diego has been special to Mexicans for hundreds of years. He was a simple peasant who is said to have seen visions of the Virgin Mary. In the Christian religion, the Virgin Mary is the mother of Jesus. According to a Mexican legend, Mary told Juan Diego that she had come to help Mexican Indians. The story of her appearance brought hope and peace to many people.

The Virgin of Guadalupe is the name given to Mary as she appeared to Juan Diego. Each Christmas season starts with a celebration in her honor. Boys dress as Juan Diego, and girls dress as an Indian woman of his time. Children come to church to be blessed by a priest and to have their picture taken in the nearby park.

◎ A merry-go-round at the carnival

◎ A fiesta dancer
shows off her
colorful costume.

After church and picture taking, it's time to have fun. At the brightly lit carnival, families eat candies, pastries, and tacos. Children laugh and shout as they zoom around in bumper cars.

That evening, Wendy lights a candle at a shrine to honor the Virgin of Guadalupe. Isuaro and Pedro walk all over the city, carrying a heavy altar with a picture of the Virgin. They arrive at the church in a silent procession. After their hard work, the boys are eager to celebrate in the park with friends.

Children carry altars through the city to honor the Virgin.

Wendy adds her candle to the dozens that others have offered.

Making special foods for the evening's fiesta

Children walk through the streets in costume.

Sparklers add light to a celebration.

LAS POSADAS

Family and friends follow Luis Angel and Ilse through the city's dark streets. The two children have been chosen to lead the first of nine nightly *posadas*. These fiestas take their name from the Spanish word for "inn."

A posada begins with children acting out the story of Mary and her husband, Joseph, on the night of Jesus' birth. Luis Angel and Ilse pretend to search for an inn where they can spend the night. They lead their group to a neighbor's house. Several people sneak in through the back door. Outdoors, the children sing a song, asking for a place to stay.

At first, the people in the house refuse to let the children in. Then Ilse tells them that Jesus is about to be born. The group is invited inside, and the celebration begins.

Everyone in the neighborhood is welcome to the posada. Even strangers may come to enjoy the fun and food. The guests feast on bean-and-cheese sandwiches, crunchy *tostadas*, and fruit punch. Children and a few lucky adults receive bags of candy, too.

Posadas take place at different homes on each of the nine nights before Christmas. Juan Carlos and Rocio go to a celebration that fills a whole street that has been shut off from traffic. Late in the evening, a *piñata* filled with treats is hung above the street. Juan Carlos swings first. Wearing a blindfold, he smacks at the piñata as a neighbor raises and lowers it.

All the guests shout out directions. "*¡Arriba! ¡Abajo! ¡Adelante!*" ("Up! Down! Straight ahead!") Juan Carlos doesn't have much luck, but an older boy breaks the piñata. The children quickly snatch the fruits and nuts that fall to the ground.

By this time, it's very late. Though the band is still playing, Rocio and Juan Carlos must go home and rest. After all, they'll have another posada to attend tomorrow night!

🌀 A neighborhood posada

◎ Juan Carlos swings at the piñata.

◎ Rocio and Juan Carlos dance to the band.

◎ Families enjoy festive music.

Angels ride in a parade as Fernando peeks out at the fiesta.

FIESTA OF THE VIRGIN OF SOLEDAD

Girls and boys in angel costumes giggle with excitement. They are riding in a parade to honor the Virgin of Soledad. *Soledad* is the Spanish word for "solitude." The Virgin of Soledad represents the Virgin Mary after the death of her son, Jesus. This parade is a serious event, so the angels' parents remind them to be calm and quiet.

Tall figures with huge, colorful heads march and dance past the parade floats. These *monos* all look different because they represent the different peoples of the world. The monos are very heavy, but eight-year-old Fernando is strong enough to wear one. Tonight he'll follow the parade to churches all over the city, walking the whole way.

⊚ Sparks fly from a tower of fireworks.

⊚ Dressed as the Virgin of Soledad, Veronica is proud to play an important part in tonight's parade.

 A nacimiento ringed by poinsettias, popular Christmas plants that are native to Mexico

The fiesta grows louder after the parade passes. A maze of vendors, food stalls, and carnival rides attracts many visitors. Nearby, workers build a tower of fireworks. Late at night, the fuses are lit. The fireworks explode in a burst of colors, and a few sparks land near the crowd. Children scream in nervous delight.

Back at home, many families set up Christmas displays called *nacimientos*. These nativity scenes show the setting of the birth of Jesus. They include colorful figures of Mary, Joseph, and many animals. For now, one figure is missing— the baby Jesus. It awaits his birthday on Christmas Day.

Anahi and her friends gather radishes to carve. Their creations will become part of a unique Oaxacan festival.

NIGHT OF THE RADISHES

In a garden on the edge of the city, Anahi works hard to unearth a radish. It's bigger than a potato, so the task takes some time. Anahi and her friends dig until they have a mountain of the red roots, both big and small. What will the children do with these strange vegetables?

Many parts of Mexico have unique Christmas fiestas. One of the most exciting events in Oaxaca is the Night of the Radishes. This tradition began more than one hundred years ago. Every year at Christmastime, Indian farmers came to the city to sell vegetables. To make their stands more attractive, the farmers carved radishes into interesting shapes. City people started buying the carvings to decorate their tables for Christmas.

Over time, radish carving became an important art in Oaxaca. Now it's the center of an entire fiesta. Thousands of people come together to see each year's carvings. The city gives prizes to the best ones by both children and adults.

Balam's two-headed monster

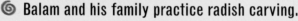

Balam and his family practice radish carving.

Like Anahi, Balam plans to enter a radish in the contest. He and his brother, Kalab, practice carving the day before the fiesta. Their parents, Claudia and Ricardo, are artists. Every year they offer many of their creations for the celebration.

The day of the fiesta, Balam attends a carving workshop for children in the city square. The radish contest will take place here tonight. Balam takes his inspiration from the strange shape of his radish. He turns it into a two-headed, dragon-like monster.

Anahi works carefully to create a traditional Oaxacan dancer. She chooses perfectly shaped radishes for the body, legs, and head. Using knives with different types of blades, she carves the dancer's face and clothes.

© Anahi creates a Oaxacan dancer.

© Small details make each carving special.

© Ricardo and Claudia proudly display their radish nacimiento.

© Ricardo with an angel carving

In the afternoon, Ricardo and Claudia arrive with more than thirty figures for the contest. Like many other artists this year, Ricardo and Claudia have created a nacimiento. Some artists have also made scenes with cornhusks or dried flowers. One figure of a woman with an oxcart took the artist over a month to make.

Each bit of color on her dress is a tiny dried flower.

As night falls, the city square fills with people. They gaze at the radishes with admiration. Later in the evening, judges award the prizes. Balam wins first place in the children's competition. His prize is a new bicycle!

 Beautiful creations for the Night of the Radishes

Jorge tosses his buñuelo bowl.

After the contest, children enjoy a dessert called *buñuelos*. These sugary, fried tortillas are served with honey. Jorge's hands get sticky as he munches on one. After he finishes eating, he takes part in another Mexican tradition. Making a wish, he tosses his buñuelo bowl to the ground, where it shatters.

Buñuelo bowls are made of pottery and are meant to be broken. Breaking old pottery at the start of the New Year is an ancient custom of Mexican Indians. It began thousands of years ago. In modern times, the smashing of the bowls celebrates the birth of the baby Jesus.

⑥ A Noche Buena parade

⑥ Karina Valeria

NOCHE BUENA

⊚ A dancing mono

Karina Valeria waves a sparkler in the air, tracing designs and watching the sparks fly. Sparklers are her favorite part of Noche Buena. This Spanish name for Christmas Eve means "Good Night." Thousands of people have come to the city square for tonight's parades.

The trumpeting of a brass band announces the first parade. At the front, a man balances a spinning wheel of fireworks on a long stick. Behind him, giant monos dance. Next come floats with children in bright costumes. Families walk alongside, carrying colored lanterns.

Giant candles light the way for a parade float.

Angels add sparkle to the celebration.

Paloma Vanessa sits atop her father's shoulders and watches it all in amazement. She laughs at the dancing monos. She doesn't mind the flying sparks or the loud noises of exploding bottle rockets. For Paloma Vanessa and many other children, this is the best show ever.

One group after another marches proudly through the city square. Some of the children on the floats toss out handfuls of candy. Children in the crowd dive between people's feet to search for the sweets.

Paloma Vanessa and her parents

◎ Marchers carefully hold a figure of the baby Jesus.

◎ A marching band

After the parades, many families go to church services. Then they share a large Christmas meal with grandparents, aunts and uncles, and cousins. One specialty of the Christmas Eve meal in Oaxaca is dried codfish. People also munch on meat-filled *tamales*, a spicy corn soup called *pozole*, and fruit salad. For dessert, there is chestnut cake, cookies, or candied pumpkin.

At midnight, families mark the birth of baby Jesus by placing his figure in their nacimientos. Children roam their neighborhoods late into the night, shooting off fireworks.

All is quiet on the next morning, December twenty-fifth. Christmas Day is called Navidad in Spanish. It's a day for resting after the many days of fiestas. Most people simply relax at home. Some children receive presents on Christmas, but others have a few more days to wait until their presents arrive.

© A complete nacimiento on the morning of Navidad

A cloth Christmas tree marks the season.

Dressing up for the fiesta

DAY OF THE THREE KINGS

 Andrea's home outside Oaxaca

Andrea lives outside Oaxaca in a little house surrounded by cornfields. On the night of January fifth, she and her cousin, Anna Laura, set their shoes outside by the door. The girls have tried to be good all year. They hope that the Three Kings will remember them.

The next morning, it's cool outside. Andrea and Anna Laura dress in warm blouses called *huipiles* that Andrea's mother has made. These traditional garments are often worn for celebrations.

When the girls open the door, they find their shoes covered with gifts and full of candy. The Three Kings have been here! Just as they brought gifts to the baby Jesus hundreds of years ago, they have visited the children of Oaxaca.

After opening the presents, the girls stuff their mouths with candy. For this fiesta, many families also serve a rich, ring-shaped bread, *rosca de reyes*. This tasty loaf has a little doll baked inside. Whoever gets the slice with the doll must host a party for everyone else on the next fiesta.

⟲ Candy and toys from the Three Kings

⟲ Andrea and Anna Laura

Another Mexican Christmas season has come to a close. Children and their families have celebrated with almost a month of parades and fiestas, dancing and fireworks. Presents and treats are important parts of Christmas in Oaxaca, but so is honoring the traditions of Mexican culture. Being with friends and family is perhaps the best of all. It's no wonder that children can't wait for the season to start all over again next December!

BUÑUELOS
A MEXICAN CHRISTMAS RECIPE

Like the children of Oaxaca, you can enjoy this delicious Christmas pastry. This recipe makes 20-24 buñuelos.

INGREDIENTS

4 cups flour

2 tablespoons sugar

1 teaspoon baking powder

2 teaspoons salt

2 eggs

¾ cup milk

¼ cup melted butter

1 cup vegetable oil *(for frying)*

½ cup sugar *(for topping)*

3 tablespoons cinnamon *(for topping)*

honey *(for topping)*

Warning:
Hot oil can cause burns.
Be sure to ask an adult
for help with this recipe.

1. Mix flour, 2 tablespoons sugar, baking powder, and salt in bowl. Stir until completely mixed.

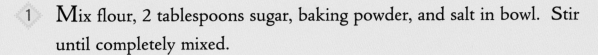

2. In another bowl, mix eggs and milk. Add to dry ingredients and stir until mixed.

3. Add melted butter. Mix until dough is easy to handle. If dough is too dry, add milk one teaspoon at a time until dough holds together.

4. Sprinkle flour lightly on a clean cutting board or countertop. Place dough on board or countertop and knead until smooth.

5. Divide dough into 20–24 pieces. Shape each piece into a ball. Place balls on board or countertop and flatten with the palm of your hand. Cover with a cloth and let stand for 20 minutes.

6. Lightly flour board or countertop again. Use a rolling pin to roll each flattened ball into a large circle, about 6 inches wide. Let stand for 5 minutes.

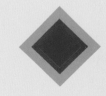

7. Ask an adult to heat 1 cup of oil in an electric skillet set at 350°. When oil is hot, the adult should fry each buñuelo until golden brown and crisp, about 3 minutes per side. Drain fried buñuelos on a paper towel.

8. While the adult fries the buñuelos, combine ½ cup sugar and cinnamon in a small bowl. Sprinkle on hot buñuelos, add honey, and eat.

SPANISH WORDS AND NAMES

¡Arriba! ¡Abajo! ¡Adelante! (ah-REE-bah ah-BAH-hoh ah-day-LAHN-tay): Up! Down! Straight ahead!

buñuelos (boon-YWAY-lohs): sweet fried pastries

fiestas (fee-EHS-tahs): celebrations

Guadalupe (gwah-dah-LOO-pay): name given to the Virgin Mary as she appeared to Juan Diego

huipiles (wee-PEE-lays): traditional woven blouses

monos (MOH-nohs): costumed parade dancers with huge, colorful heads

nacimientos (NAH-see-mee-ehn-tohs): Christmas scenes with figures that portray the scene of the birth of Jesus

Navidad (NAH-vee-dahd): Christmas Day

Noche Buena (NOH-chay BWAY-nah): Christmas Eve

Oaxaca (wuh-HAH-kah): a city in southern Mexico

piñata (pee-NYAH-tah): a decorated pot, filled with treats, for breaking at a party

posadas (poh-SAH-dahs): celebrations held on the nine nights before Christmas

pozole (poh-SOH-lay): spicy soup made with corn

rosca de reyes (ROHS-kah DAY RAY-yehs): "Kings' ring," or sweet bread eaten on the Day of the Three Kings

Soledad (SOH-lay-dahd): solitude

tamales (tah-MAH-lays): meat rolled in cornmeal dough and steamed

tostadas (toh-STAH-dahs): fried dough with beans or other toppings

FURTHER READING

Ancona, George. *The Piñata Maker/El Piñatero*. New York: Harcourt, 1994. Color photographs and text in both English and Spanish describe the craft of piñata making.

De Paola, Tomie. *The Night of Las Posadas*. New York: Putnam, 1999. In this picture book, a miracle helps make a posada celebration possible in Santa Fe, New Mexico.

Hoyt-Goldsmith, Diane. *Las Posadas: An Hispanic Christmas Celebration*. New York: Holiday House, 1999. A Mexican American girl celebrates the nine posadas with traditional treats, music, and costumes.

Kelley, Emily. *Christmas Around the World*. Minneapolis: Carolrhoda Books, 1986. Text and illustrations describe the Christmas traditions of many countries, including Mexico.

INDEX